beyou

A 30 day devotional

Casey Treat

WINTERS
PUBLISHING GROUP

Scripture text is taken from the New King James Version (NKJV) unless otherwise specified.

This book is designed to provide accurate and authoritative information with regard to the subject matter covered. This information is given with the understanding that neither the author nor Winters Publishing, LLC is engaged in rendering legal, professional advice. Since the details of your situation are fact dependent, you should additionally seek the services of a competent professional.

The opinions expressed by the author are not necessarily those of Winters Publishing, LLC.

Published by Winters Publishing, LLC
2448 E. 81st St. Suite #4802 | Tulsa, Oklahoma 74137 USA

Book design copyright © 2015 by Winters Publishing, LLC. All rights reserved.
Cover design by Joana Quilantang and Christian Faith Center
Interior design by Caypeeline Casas

Published in the United States of America

ISBN: 978-1-68207-700-9
1. Religion / Inspirational
2. Self-Help / Motivational & Inspirational
15.10.09

You know that God designed you, created you, and loves you. But, do you really believe it? For most of us our doubts, fears, and the challenges of life cause us to wonder if God really loves us. Insecurities cause us to question who we are and how we can succeed in life. Many wonder, "What is my calling and purpose; and what do I have to do to be happy and fulfilled?" If you will walk with me for the next 30 days through the pages of this devotional, you will find these answers, and you will be on your way to a more fulfilling life. Wherever you are at today, God wants to move you forward and lift you up in every realm. Each day we will look at what the Lord says about you; how to make it practical and powerful; and how to see real change in your life. God did create you, and He does love you. When you can be the person He designed you to be and love yourself as He does, you'll be on your way. In 30 days, you can start a new habit of thinking and move to a new place in destiny. Let's do it together. God believes in you, I believe in you, now it's time that you believe and...

be*you*

#1: God Named YOU

Before I was born the Lord called me; from my
mother's womb he has spoken my name.

Isaiah 49:1 (NIV)

Be YOU. The real YOU. The YOU God named from your mother's womb. Nothing more, nothing less. Because only when you are freely being the authentic YOU God created, will you thrive in this life. Only the true YOU will be able to fully prosper in your soul and in every realm of life. But, how do you get there? Is it even possible to get there? This is what these next 30 days will be about. Simply you becoming–YOU. For some, you'll be rediscovering YOU. For others, you'll be uncovering new thoughts about YOU that you've never known. And for others, you'll be going deeper and building upon a great foundation of YOU.

"Be YOU" is about believing that everything from your personality, to your gifts, to your physical make-up was God's idea. It's about knowing God loves and values you right now; and if you never did anything else for Him, He would still love you and be proud to call you His child. It's about learning how to shed the negative layers and "names" the world has piled on you so that you can own the original and ideal YOU God designed you to be. It's about learning to love your uniqueness, imperfections and quirks. It's about not judging your missteps or failures, but instead, using them as platforms for your destiny.

This BE YOU devotional is not about you striving to become something "better" or pressing to achieve something you've never done before. It's not about perfection, and it's not about performance. It's simply about peeling off of YOU anything that is not God's plan for you; letting go of those things that cloud who you really are, and those things that burden you, weigh you down or slow your walk.

So relax and take a deep breath. These next 30 days will lift you, encourage you, build you, and heal you. You will learn to love and accept yourself in a deeper way. You will learn to let go of all those expectations that God has never asked you to live up to, and simply learn to BE YOU. It's is all about celebrating YOU. The YOU you are today.

BELIEVE IT

Today, meditate on the fact that before the foundation of the earth, God knew your name. He thought of you, and He created you to be YOU.

SAY IT

Father, I believe the me You created is the perfect me. Thank You for working in my life during these next 30 days as I study Your Word and learn to embrace the me You created me to be!

READ IT

Your hands have made me and fashioned me, an intricate unity. Job 10:8

You watched me as I was being formed in utter seclusion, as I was woven together in the dark of the womb. Psalm 139:15 (NLT)

Even before the world was made, God had already chosen us to be his through our union with Christ, so that we would be holy and without fault before him. Ephesians 1:4 (GNT)

_____

_____

_____

_____

_____

_____

_____

_____

_____

_____

_____

_____

#2: The Real YOU is Like Him

Then God said, "Let Us make man in Our image,
according to Our likeness…"

Genesis 1:26

To be YOU, to know who the real YOU is, you must go back to the very beginning. You must come to believe that you were God's idea; and because of His great desire for you to *be*, He created YOU. It's an awesome thought: You are a creation of God!

You were on God's mind long before you were born. He loved you deeply and chose you to be His child. Not only that, you were expertly designed by the same hands that created the countless stars, the mountains and the seas, and all the creatures in them. There is so much comfort in knowing this because you realize you don't have to create yourself. You don't have to carry the stress of trying to carve out your own path and destiny. If you will believe God fashioned you with a plan and a purpose, you can rest in the truth that the real you, and all the details of your life, are found in your relationship with Him.

But God doesn't stop there. Not only were you created by Him, you were made to be like Him. He breathed His very life into you. YOU are a divine person with a divine purpose and life to live. This is a huge truth that seems too good to be true, doesn't it? You might look at your life right now and say, "This does not look like God!" We've all had times when we've thought that. Nevertheless, God's Word is true, and as you walk with Him daily and come to know Him more deeply, this reality will become bigger and more real in your life.

BELIEVE IT

Today, meditate on these truths: Believe you were created by the same God that created the heavens and the earth. Think about the fact that you are not just a mammal; you are a dynamic person with gifts and talents and opportunities that have been prepared and planned out just for you to walk in!

SAY IT

Father, I believe You are God, Creator, and Lord. Thank You for loving me, for choosing me and for speaking Your life into me. I believe I am created in Your image to live a life of purpose and significance. You've perfectly designed

ME to be unique and wonderful, and I embrace the fullness of who You created me to be.

READ IT

Every day of my life was recorded in your book. Every moment was laid out before a single day had passed. Psalm 139:16 (NLT)

For whom He foreknew, He also predestined to be conformed to the image of His Son... Romans 8:29

Being confident of this very thing, that He who has begun a good work in you will complete it until the day of Jesus Christ. Philippians 1:6

#3: Be YOU...Without Any Add-Ons

> *But whoever did want (Jesus), who believed he was*
> *who he claimed and would do what he said, He made*
> *to be their true selves, their child-of-God selves.*
>
> *John 1:12 (Message)*

When a gifted sculptor creates a sculpture, it is a beautiful work of art to behold. But then, if someone comes by and adds on a coat to it... then a bag... then a blanket... and then perhaps smears a little mud on it, suddenly it is changed. It doesn't look at all how it was meant to look. The sculptor himself might not even recognize his own creation!

Yesterday we read that YOU were created in the likeness and image of God. That image, that "sculpture," is the real YOU. The core of who you are is the thumbprint of God Himself; and His character, thoughts, and ways have been carved into the depths of your heart. But, for many of us, the world has come along and clipped some add-ons to that sculpture: things like anger, fear, depression, eating disorders, constant worry, lust, or pride. Over time, we accept these add-ons as part of who we are, forgetting they were never part of God's original sculpture.

Jesus came to remind each of us who we really are. He came to, once again, make YOU your true self… your child-of-God self. He came to show you that anything outside the original plan of being made in God's image is simply an add-on, nothing more. So, that depression you've struggled with for so long and accepted as part of who you are? Yeah, that's not really you. It's just an add-on. And that anorexia? Or that anger? Or that failure? Those things are just add-ons. And, the great thing about add-ons is that they can become take-offs!

You might have been carrying some of these add-ons around a long time, so it'll be a process to free yourself of them completely. But know this: YOU, the core of YOU, is created in God's image. And this *Be You* Devotional is all about helping you to get back to that original design, and to rally you to turn all those add-ons into take-offs!

BELIEVE IT

Any part of you that isn't made in the image of God and His character is simply an add-on. Accept that these things are not YOU, and they don't have to be a part of your identity. You can Be YOU without those trappings. Ask God to help you.

SAY IT

Father, I believe You have given me the power and desire to be that original sculpture, a person made in Your image. I believe I am full of life and power. Help me to walk in strength and integrity so I can let go of any add-ons in my life.

READ IT

Throw off your old sinful nature and your former way of life, which is corrupted by lust and deception. Ephesians 4:22 (NLT)

Put off the old man with his deeds. Colossian 3:9

For God has not given us a spirit of fear, but of power and of love and of a sound mind. 2 Timothy 1:7

CASEY TREAT

_____

_____

_____

_____

_____

_____

_____

_____

_____

_____

_____

_____

#4: The Vision of YOU

Where there is no vision, the people perish.

Proverbs 29:18 (KJV)

Vision is a dynamic life force. It's a spiritual power that gives you the ability to see by faith, even those things that you cannot see with your natural eye. In fact, I believe what you see when your eyes are closed is far more important than what you see when they are open. Your vision of the real YOU cannot be who you see reflected in the mirror, because that "you" will morph and change as you go through life. No, the vision of the authentic YOU is who you see with the eyes of your heart.

Who do you see when you close your eyes? Be brutally honest. Then believe, whoever that is, that God loves you unconditionally, right here, right now. Just the way you are. And, if you never changed a thing, God would still love you completely. Let your vision for YOU start there. You are a child loved wholly and outrageously by God. This is where the real YOU begins.

So many people are perishing in this world because they don't have this vision. They don't believe there is a God who loves them so much, that even before they did anything to deserve it, He gave His only Son to die just so they could be reunited into fellowship with Him. Maybe the reason some reading this devotional have felt their "real YOU" has been perishing is because they've never let this reality sink into the core of their vision. Maybe this is you?

Yes, there may be aspects of YOU that you struggle with right now. But instead of diving into the next self-help program, spend some quality time learning to believe that God's love is authentic, powerful, and personal towards YOU. Get a vision of YOU being favored and accepted by an unmatchable Father in Heaven. This is where the real YOU begins.

BELIEVE IT

Meditate today about how God's love is for YOU personally, specifically, and intimately. Allow that truth to roll around in your mind and heart until that vision becomes vividly clear. This might take some time, but it's well worth it!

SAY IT

Father, I believe and accept Your love for me. You loved me before I did anything to deserve it, You love me now, even when I make mistakes, and You will love me for eternity.

Thank You that You help me to build this vision as a foundation for my life.

READ IT

Then God said, "Let Us make man in Our image, according to Our likeness; let them have dominion over the fish of the sea, over the birds of the air, and over the cattle, over all the earth and over every creeping thing that creeps on the earth." So God created man in His own image; in the image of God He created him; male and female He created them. Genesis 1:26-27

Brethren, I do not count myself to have apprehended; but one thing I do, forgetting those things which are behind and reaching forward to those things which are ahead, I press toward the goal for the prize of the upward call of God in Christ Jesus. Philippians 3:13-14

_____

_____

_____

_____

_____

_____

_____

_____

_____

_____

_____

_____

_____

#5: Everything About YOU is Good

For we are God's [own] handiwork (His workman-
ship), recreated in Christ Jesus, [born anew] that
we may do those good works which God predestined
(planned beforehand) for us [taking paths which He
prepared ahead of time], that we should walk in them
[living the good life which He prearranged and made
ready for us to live].

Ephesians 2:10 (AMP)

Everything about YOU is good. How can it not be? God Himself fashioned every aspect of you: your physical features, your personality, your gifts and your talents. He even carefully planned out a destiny that would be full of His blessings, and that would satisfy you to the very core. When you believe this and begin to trust God in this, you can take a deep sigh of relief. You can relax knowing that the life He planned for YOU is a good life, filled with good works that God prepared beforehand just for you.

To be you, you don't have to strive and struggle. To be you, you don't have to try and be something else. And even better, you don't have to scrap and battle to find your own course. You simply need to walk in the path God already created for you. On the other hand, it is important to realize that just because God prepared your path, this does not mean everything in your life will come easily. Your destiny is not just going to drop out of the sky. You're going to have to work hard for it, stretch your faith for it, and utilize all your gifts and talents to pursue it.

For some reading this right now, your life does not look like something God would have planned. Maybe because of your own choices, or maybe because of circumstances beyond your control, you find yourself in difficulty and pain. Here's the amazing thing about God: it's never too late to be what you want to be. God is that big, that good, that powerful. He can take any shipwrecked life and turn it into something beautiful. But, you have to trust Him and be patient. It won't be easy, but it will be so worth it!

Today, right now, YOU are good! How could a loving God make anything else?

BELIEVE IT

Think on God's goodness and thank Him for all the great things He's done in your life. Meditate on the aspects of YOU that you love, knowing you never need to be anything except the authentic YOU.

SAY IT

I believe You have planned a good destiny for me, a great life full of all that You are. I trust in You, God, to lead and guide me toward the blessed life You have for me.

READ IT

His lord said to him, "Well done, good and faithful servant; you were faithful over a few things, I will make you ruler over many things. Enter into the joy of your lord." Matthew 25:21

The thief does not come except to steal, and to kill, and to destroy. I have come that they may have life, and that they may have it more abundantly. John 10:10

#6: YOU are Valuable

The Son of Man did not come to be served, but to serve,
and to give His life a ransom for many.

Matthew 20:28

YOU are extremely valuable to God! Think about it: The God of the Universe was so unsatisfied with having an estranged life with you that He sent His only Son to die... just so that YOU could be restored to Him! It's an awesome thought that takes much time and meditation to actually wrap your mind and heart around it. But it is true.

So much of "religion" teaches us that we are not worthy, that we have to get ourselves together to receive from God, but that's not the case. Before the world was saved, before any person could get himself together (as if that would've been possible anyway), Jesus came and died for all mankind. This thought can bring such relief to your soul because you can know that RIGHT NOW, you are enough. You will not be more worthy once you develop more spiritual maturity, clean up your life, give more to the church...you are enough today. He died for you before you did a thing for

Him, and your value to Him does not depend on anything you will ever do or achieve in the future.

God paid a huge price for you and for me. It's important to remind ourselves of this on a regular basis. The spirit of the world relentlessly impresses on us that we have to be "as good as…" or "as successful as…" or "as pretty as…" It's a ploy of the enemy to keep us frustrated and feeling like we will never measure up to a standard that can never be attained. God is not asking YOU to measure up to anything. Just Be YOU. Embrace and accept who you are today. Sure, we all want to move forward and "be better." Just make sure the image you are reaching for is who you are in Christ. There you will find your true value. There you will find rest.

BELIEVE IT

Meditate on God's love for you. Not when you fix yourself, but His unconditional love for who you are today. Agree with that love and thank God for it.

SAY IT

Father, I believe You loved me and came for me, even before I could do anything to deserve it. Thank You for Jesus and the price He paid. I will live knowing all that You gave for me to be a part of Your heart.

READ IT

But the other, answering, rebuked him, saying, "Do you not even fear God, seeing you are under the same condemnation? And we indeed justly, for we receive the due reward of our deeds; but this Man has done nothing wrong." Then he said to Jesus, "Lord, remember me when You come into Your kingdom." And Jesus said to him, "Assuredly, I say to you, today you will be with Me in Paradise." Luke 23:40-43

Whatever I tell you in the dark, speak in the light; and what you hear in the ear, preach on the housetops. And do not fear those who kill the body but cannot kill the soul. But rather fear Him who is able to destroy both soul and body in hell. Are not two sparrows sold for a copper coin? And not one of them falls to the ground apart from your Father's will. But the very hairs of your head are all numbered. Do not fear therefore; you are of more value than many sparrows. Matthew 10:27-31

_____

_____

_____

_____

_____

_____

_____

_____

_____

_____

_____

_____

_____

#7: YOU Have a Purpose

> *And we know that all things work together for good to those who love God, to those who are the called according to His purpose. For whom He foreknew, He also predestined to be conformed to the image of His Son, that He might be the firstborn among many brethren.*
>
> *Romans 8:28-29*

Every person is called according to God's purpose. Yes, that means YOU! God has called you to a destiny and a life that He planned for you. God isn't controlling your life; rather, He knows your gifts, your desires, your capacity and based on this, He designed the perfect destiny just for YOU. This includes your marriage, family, career, ministry, friends and areas of influence.

In addition, when you are walking in your purpose, loving God and serving God, all things work together for your good! What an incredible promise! No matter what hardships or negative circumstances come your way, you can rest assured that God is working on your behalf to bring good things out of any adversity.

What specifically is God's purpose for your life? It's right up there in the scripture. His purpose for your life is to be conformed to the image of His Son. Because this is the real YOU. This is the best YOU. And this, is the YOU that you deeply desire to be.

You become conformed to His image as you pray and read the Bible, and as you meditate on God's promises. This is why this 30-day devotional is so important to complete! As you grow each day, becoming more and more like Jesus, your fears will melt away, your worries and anxieties will decrease, the emotional pains from failure and loss will begin to dissolve, and you will experience the true soul prosperity God desires for you to have.

You have a purpose. It's to be like Jesus. It's to BE YOU!

BELIEVE IT

Be conscious today to be like Jesus. Meditate on Jesus' words and begin to renew your mind to the mind of Christ. Relax and rest assured that as God's Word is working in you, you are becoming more like Him.

SAY IT

Father, I believe You have predestined me to be able to become more like Jesus every day. Holy Spirit, help me to have the mind of Christ and to walk today as Jesus walked. Help me to be the hands and feet of Jesus to those around me.

READ IT

Furthermore, because we are united with Christ, we have received an inheritance from God, for he chose us in advance, and he makes everything work out according to his plan. Ephesians 1:11 (NLT)

"For I know the plans I have for you," says the Lord. "They are plans for good and not for disaster, to give you a future and a hope." Jeremiah 29:11 (NLT)

If the whole body were an eye, how would you hear? Or if your whole body were an ear, how would you smell anything? But our bodies have many parts, and God has put each part just where he wants it. How strange a body would be if it had only one part! Yes, there are many parts, but only one body. The eye can never say to the hand, "I don't need you." The head can't say to the feet, "I don't need you." In fact, some parts of the body that seem weakest and least important are actually the most necessary. 1 Corinthians 12:17-22 (NLT)

_____

_____

_____

_____

_____

_____

_____

_____

_____

_____

_____

_____

#8: YOU are Found in Jesus

Remain in me, and I will remain in you. For a branch cannot produce fruit if it is severed from the vine, and you cannot be fruitful unless you remain in me.

John 15:4 (NLT)

Have you ever hung around someone who made you a better you? Even by just being around their positivity for a little while, you find yourself thinking up, speaking up, dreaming up. You feel like the best YOU. And then there's the friend that isn't quite like this. When you are around them, even for a few moments, you find yourself saying things you know you shouldn't, doing things you wish you wouldn't, and taking on funky attitudes that get you nowhere fast.

Jesus knew we would be greatly influenced by the people we spend the most time with, which is why He invites us to remain in Him constantly. Just as a branch can only flourish if it is joined to the vine, you can only be the best YOU when you make a conscious effort daily to abide in Christ. This simply means to be aware of His presence and His power working in your life. It means to trust in His wisdom and provision for all your concerns and needs. It means to spend time every day meditating on His Word and His promises.

If we hang around the spirit of this world, we will live down, discouraged, and depressed. But if we will abide in Christ, "hang with Jesus," His Spirit will lift ours up, and we will have the ability to keep our attitudes positive and full of hope, no matter what comes our way.

Walk with Jesus today. Be aware of His presence in your life. Tune into His Spirit and attitude so you can be strengthened on the inside throughout this day.

BELIEVE IT

Is there an issue or an area of your life that is troubling you? Talk to Jesus about it today. Find some quiet time to rest in His presence, and He will speak to your heart. Believe His promises about that issue, and peace will guard your heart and mind.

SAY IT

Jesus, I believe You are with me always. I believe I can abide in Your presence throughout this day, and draw on the power of Your Spirit that lives on the inside of me. Thank You for Your unending love and friendship.

READ IT

Jesus told him, "I am the way, the truth, and the life. No one can come to the Father except through me." John 14:6 (NLT)

I can do all things through Christ who strengthens me. Philippians 4:13

Whoever has the Son has life; whoever does not have the Son of God does not have life. 1 John 5:12 (NIV)

#9: Choose YOU

I call heaven and earth as witnesses today against you,
that I have set before you life and death, blessing and
cursing; therefore choose life.

Deuteronomy 30:19

Choice. It's the most miraculous and powerful gift God gave us. Humans are the only species on planet earth that operate outside the confines of instinct and habit. We are the only beings that can remember our past and choose how we are going to think about it. We hold the power to choose who we want to become, what we want to think and feel, and whom we want to serve. And, because of this gift, you can choose to be YOU...the YOU you dreamt of as a kid, the YOU you know you can be, the YOU God created you to become.

One of the greatest hindrances to choosing to be YOU is dealing with all the aspects and issues life has thrown at you up until this point. The dad who told you you'd never amount to anything. The friend who hurt you. The poverty you were born into. The divorce. The failure. The abuse. The sickness. The fear. The depression. The list could go on and on. Yes, we live in a broken state of humanity, and, unfortunately, some of us have come face-to-face with some tough challenges, many of which were beyond our control. And so you stopped dreaming. And you stopped going after the YOU you know is inside your heart.

Yes, there have been things that have happened that were beyond your control. But don't allow those things you cannot control make you give up on what you can control. Today, no matter where you are in life and no matter what challenges you have faced, it's time to make a life-changing choice: Choose to Be YOU anyway! God has set before you life and death…choose LIFE. Choose the life God designed just for YOU. Choose life in your mind and emotions. Choose how you will respond from this day forward, and choose how you will think about YOU from now on.

Make a stand today…Choose to BE YOU!

BELIEVE IT

Reflect today on any area of your life where you believe you are a victim of circumstance. Re-think that belief. What can you choose to think about it? How can you choose to respond? Today, choose life in your thoughts, responses, and words.

SAY IT

Father, I believe You have made me a sovereign being with Your Spirit of power residing in me. I choose not to be a victim; rather, I choose how I'll respond to and feel about every circumstance. Thank You for helping me to be authentically ME.

READ IT

Do not conform to the pattern of this world, but be transformed by the renewing of your mind. Then you will be able to test and approve what God's will is—his good, pleasing and perfect will. Romans 12:2 (NIV)

I praise you because I am fearfully and wonderfully made. Psalm 139:14 (NIV)

Are not two sparrows sold for a penny? Yet not one of them will fall to the ground outside your Father's care. And even the very hairs of your head are all numbered. So don't be afraid; you are worth more than many sparrows. Matthew 10:29-31(NIV)

_____

_____

_____

_____

_____

_____

_____

_____

_____

_____

_____

_____

#10: YOU are Called—Part 1

Behold what manner of love the Father has bestowed
on us, that we should be called children of God!

1 John 3:1

What does it mean to be "called?" To be the YOU God called you to be, you must first understand that God places the significance and value on YOU, not on your job or your ministry or your achievements. YOU are extremely precious to God and He has called you first and foremost to be adopted into His family. He loves you dearly, and infinitely more than any earthly father could love his children. You cannot become more "called" than that.

You are not called to be a "position," you are called to be a child of God; and out of THAT calling, your life springs forth. It's not what you DO that's important, it's WHO you are. And, this is the whole message of BE YOU...you embracing the true YOU. Not you doing things to try and become the YOU you think you need to be.

In our culture, even in the church world, there is a man-made perspective that creates a hierarchy of certain callings being more important or more valuable to God than others. But, that's not God's perspective at all. There is no cast system; there is no calling that is higher or one that is lower. There is no job or position that is "more" of God than another. In fact, God even said that if you so much as give a drink of water to a prophet, you will receive that prophet's reward. To God, the calling of the prophet is the same as the person who is called to serve and supply provision for that prophet. The rewards are the same!

When you are living to love God with all your heart, you are in your calling. When you are on a passionate pursuit to know Jesus and become like Him, you are in your calling. When you are fully embracing the YOU God designed you to be, you are in your calling. Never underestimate that. Never devalue that. Remember, YOU are enough; right here, right now! And God is proud of YOU!

BELIEVE IT

Meditate today on the promise that YOU have been specifically chosen by God to be His precious child. He loves you outrageously and cannot possibly love you any more than He does right now. You don't have to earn His love; you simply need to believe and receive it.

SAY IT

Father, I believe that You love me, that You chose me, and that You called me to be an important part of Your family. Help me to embrace Your love in a deeper way today. Help me to believe it so that I can be used by You to share Your love with others.

READ IT

And we know that all things work together for good to those who love God, to those who are the called according to His purpose. Romans 8:28

As His divine power has given to us all things that pertain to life and godliness, through the knowledge of Him who called us by glory and virtue. 2 Peter 1:3

And it shall come to pass that whoever calls on the name of the Lord shall be saved. For in Mount Zion and in Jerusalem there shall be deliverance, as the Lord has said, Among the remnant whom the Lord calls. Joel 2:32

_____

_____

_____

_____

_____

_____

_____

_____

_____

_____

_____

_____

_____

#11: YOU are Called—Part 2

But you are a chosen generation, a royal priesthood, a holy nation, His own special people, that you may proclaim the praises of Him who called you out of darkness into His marvelous light.

1 Peter 2:9

So many people hear the word "calling" and think, "I'm not called because I'm not in the ministry." Guess what? You are called because you are in the ministry! Granted, your ministry might be as a teacher in a high school, as a businessperson in the marketplace, or as a soldier fighting for our nation. Your ministry may be as a spouse, as a parent, as a grandparent, as a friend, and well...basically as a person interfacing with the human race. In other words, wherever you are, that's where your ministry is.

You were chosen to be a royal priesthood, a holy nation, God's own special people. And out of that calling comes your ministry, which is to be a voice of praise for the God who called you out of the darkness into His marvelous light! You have been called so that you can now walk with God and share the message of Jesus through your example on this earth. Every time you touch the life of another, you are ministering within your individual calling.

God saved YOU for this time in history. You could have been born at any time and at any place, but you are here now. You are a part of His Church and a part of His story. You are a very special person in His special plan. You are called, and you are chosen. Live today with the outrageous confidence in the YOU God has called you to be. Whatever your season in life, whatever your job, whatever your influence, live strong and be bold to proclaim the praises of your God. THIS IS YOUR CALLING!

BELIEVE IT

Own your calling today. Look around you and recognize the people God has placed within your sphere of influence. How can you reach out to them today and share the message of Christ? It might be in a smile, an encouraging word, an invitation to church, or an offer to pray for them. Be bold and very courageous, knowing your God has gone before you to minister to those around you.

SAY IT

Father, I believe You have saved me for a time such as this. Thank You for equipping me and preparing me for my calling today. Help me today to discern Your voice as You lead and guide me in my ministry and as I influence the people You have placed within my sphere. Thank You for calling me to such a wonderful life.

READ IT

I, therefore, the prisoner of the Lord, beseech you to walk worthy of the calling with which you were called, with all lowliness and gentleness, with longsuffering, bearing with one another in love, endeavoring to keep the unity of the Spirit in the bond of peace. Ephesians 4:1-3

Now all things are of God, who has reconciled us to Himself through Jesus Christ, and has given us the ministry of reconciliation, that is, that God was in Christ reconciling the world to Himself, not imputing their trespasses to them, and has committed to us the word of reconciliation. 2 Corinthians 5:18-19

But as many as received Him, to them He gave the right to become children of God, to those who believe in His name. John 1:12

#12: YOU are Different...and That's a Good Thing

> *Your body has many parts—limbs, organs, cells—but*
> *no matter how many parts you can name, you're*
> *still one body. It's all the different-but-similar parts*
> *arranged and functioning together. If Ear said, "I'm*
> *not beautiful like Eye, limpid and expressive; I don't*
> *deserve a place on the head," would you want to*
> *remove it from the body? If the body was all eye, how*
> *could it hear? If all ear, how could it smell? As it is, we*
> *see that God has carefully placed each part of the body*
> *right where he wanted it.*
>
> *1 Corinthians 12:12, 14,16-18 (Message)*

Have you ever been in a group of people and thought, "Man, I feel so different from all these guys; I don't think the same way; I don't find the same things funny; I feel like I don't fit in"? We've all felt this at some point. And then usually, our way of dealing with it is to try and conform to be like them, because different is bad, right? No! In fact, different is exactly what God wants from every single one of us.

Think about the Bible. From Genesis to Revelation, the scriptures encompass thousands of years and tell the stories of hundreds of kings, priests, regular Joe's, orphans, servants, widows, and so many more. Are any of these real-life characters exactly the same as another? Not even close! And yet, God chose to use each and every one of them individually because of their individuality.

Jesus is looking for different. We saw it in His choice of His followers during His ministry on earth, and we certainly see it today inside the church. He needs you to Be YOU because that YOU is exactly what is required to fulfill your true calling. If you are trying to conform to someone else, then you'll actually disqualify yourself from everything God has for you.

Are you different? Good! That's exactly what God wants you to be. Find value in your diversity and use it to your advantage! Own YOUR gifts, YOUR calling, and YOUR personality…and be YOU to the fullest!

BELIEVE IT

Do you feel insecure about parts of your personality? Instead of trying to change yourself, what if you embraced your individuality? See your uniqueness as a gift, not a curse, and simply be YOU.

SAY IT

Father, I believe You have made me different from any other person, and those differences are exactly what You will use to reach people. Help me to embrace every aspect of *me* today.

READ IT

Therefore, if anyone is in Christ, he is a new creation; old things have passed away; behold, all things have become new. 2 Corinthians 5:17

For in Christ Jesus neither circumcision nor uncircumcision avails anything, but a new creation. Galatians 6:15

Every good gift and every perfect gift is from above, and comes down from the Father of lights, with whom there is no variation or shadow of turning. James 1:17

_____

_____

_____

_____

_____

_____

_____

_____

_____

_____

_____

_____

_____

#13: Be YOU: The Overcomer

> *Then God said, "Let Us make man in Our image,*
> *according to Our likeness; let them have dominion over*
> *the fish of the sea, over the birds of the air, and over the*
> *cattle, over all the earth and over every creeping thing*
> *that creeps on the earth."*
>
> *Genesis 1:26*

Dominion. That's a pretty unusual word nowadays to describe ourselves, isn't it? Not many of us are walking around each day thinking we are taking dominion of anything. But, I really believe if you can learn to absorb this concept into your heart and mind, it will help you to believe you are who God says you are…to own the fact that God's original intent was for you to have dominion in every area of your life.

If you stop and think about it, man has taken dominion over this earth. We've created ways to use its resources, to subdue the animals, to reap from the land, to travel around the globe, to go where we want to go and do what we want to do. But this scripture isn't simply talking about having dominion over our natural world. God is communicating a spirit to us, a way of thinking.

To be the YOU God envisioned, you've got to believe He has called you to have dominion and to be an overcomer. But, don't let the bigness of these words intimidate you. This simply means that whatever you are facing today—a difficult situation at work, an addiction, a challenge in your marriage, or the pressure of financial strain—you can walk through that adversity with the power of God. Rather than seeing yourself as a victim, God wants you to draw on His strength and His courage within you so that you can see yourself winning.

Having dominion today simply means choosing patience over frustration. It's saying the kind word to your spouse or child when you really want to speak words of anger. It's releasing your fears to God and choosing to trust Him instead of allowing yourself to be bound up inside with worry. You can walk with dominion in your life. You just have to believe you are an overcomer.

BELIEVE IT

Is there an area in your life that is weighing you down? Today, see yourself walking through it as an overcomer. Don't focus on tomorrow; just picture your victory today. Then make a choice today that will help you take a step forward.

SAY IT

Father, I believe Your life, Spirit, and strength are working in me. You created me to have dominion in my life, and to walk on top of the stress and pressure that comes my way. Thank You for leading and guiding me to a place of victory.

READ IT

Yet in all these things we are more than conquerors through Him who loved us. Romans 8:37

I can do all things through Christ who strengthens me. Philippians 4:13

You are of God, little children, and have overcome them, because He who is in you is greater than he who is in the world. 1 John 4:4

_____

_____

_____

_____

_____

_____

_____

_____

_____

_____

_____

_____

#14: YOU Can Have Hope—Part 1

*May the God of your hope so fill you with all joy and
peace in believing [through the experience of your
faith] that by the power of the Holy Spirit you may
abound and be overflowing (bubbling over) with hope.*

Romans 15:13 (AMP)

Hope is a powerful force. Hope will motivate you toward
the greatest life possible. Hope will propel you to be YOU.
Hope looks at the outward circumstances and believes in
the promises of God. When the economy is down, when
the report is negative, or when the marriage is bad, hope
says, "All of this can change. God is good and He's going to
help me through this to get to a brighter tomorrow." Hope
is a vital component you must possess along your journey
of being YOU.

When I was a teenager, I had no hope. My life was
visionless and I didn't believe anything would ever change.
I was completely hopeless. So, I medicated my pain through
an endless cycle of drug use. And then one day, I met my
spiritual father, Julius Young. He looked up at me and said,
"Big Red, you can change." I don't know why or how those

words made such an impact on my life, but when I heard them, all of a sudden hope was birthed in my heart. Hope hit me and I began to believe my life could change. One year later, I was in Bible school, and shortly after that I met Wendy. I'm so glad my life intersected with Julius and with the hope of God.

Whatever area of your life, big or small, that seems hopeless, let me assure you: God is your source of hope. And, He will fill you completely with joy and peace when you trust in Him. No matter how big that hopelessness might appear to be, God is bigger. He's big enough to overflow that emptiness with His powerful force of hope. If He did it for me, when I was a rebellious drug addict, He will most certainly do it for you. Hope in God. You can trust Him.

BELIEVE IT

We all have times when we lose sight of our hope, so it's important to know what things can generate hope in our lives. What is a hope catalyst for you? Is it a certain scripture? An uplifting song? A walk in nature? A long workout? Identify those things that help you restore hope in your heart, and engage in one of those today!

SAY IT

Father, I believe You are my source of hope. I believe You can bring change to those areas of my life where I have given up hope. Help me today to trust in You. Help me to see through Your eyes of hope.

READ IT

Why am I discouraged? Why is my heart so sad? I will put my hope in God! I will praise him again— my Savior and my God! Psalm 43:5 (NLT)

Where there is no vision, the people perish. Proverbs 29:18 (KJV)

Let us who are of the day be sober, putting on the breastplate of faith and love, and as a helmet the hope of salvation. 1 Thessalonians 5:8

_____

_____

_____

_____

_____

_____

_____

_____

_____

_____

_____

_____

_____

#15: You Can Have Hope—Part 2

Hope deferred makes the heart sick, but when the desire comes, it is a tree of life.

Proverbs 13:12

This is a powerful scripture that teaches us the force that hope has in our lives. When hope comes to pass, it is a tree of life! But when hope is deferred, it makes our hearts sick. To be a healthy, thriving YOU, you must understand the potential of hope and learn to harness it correctly in your life.

Hope is a motor for your life. Whatever you put your hope in creates a significant force of movement, so it's vital you know how to aim your hope in the right way. If you direct your hope toward the things of God, you will experience a prosperous soul. But, if you set your hope on things God has never asked you to set your hope on, even if you attain those things, eventually your soul will grow disillusioned and sick. Those hopes will break your heart.

Today let's take a look at WHAT you are to hope for. Hope, Biblically-speaking, is an internal faith in God, a belief that God is good and that He loves us. We are to use the force of hope to set our hearts on the promises of God found in His scriptures: His healing, His salvation, His provision, the forgiveness that comes through Jesus, the promise of eternal life, and blessing on our marriage and family. This is what hope was made for. These hopes are infallible and will always be a tree of life for us.

Is there a particular promise in God's Word that applies to your circumstances today? Then fully set your hope on that promise, because it will be an anchor for your soul. And always remember: most things we hope for don't happen as quickly as we want them to. God's Word is true and His timing is always perfect.

BELIEVE IT

Are you experiencing a hope deferred? First, make sure you've set your hope on the right thing. Talk with a mature Christian if you need some advice. Second, get in agreement with another and pray. Allow this partnership to encourage you. Third, be patient and don't grow weary in well-doing, for at the right time, you will reap a harvest if you do not give up. Meditate on Galatians 6:9.

SAY IT

Father, I believe You are directing my hopes, and that You give me the desires of my heart. I will trust in You completely to bring Your promises to pass in my life.

READ IT

We have this hope as an anchor for our lives. It is safe and sure. Hebrews 6:19 (GNT)

Let us hold fast the confession of our hope without wavering, for He who promised is faithful. Hebrews 10:23

Therefore, with minds that are alert and fully sober, set your hope on the grace to be brought to you when Jesus Christ is revealed at his coming. 1 Peter 1:13 (NIV)

And let us not grow weary while doing good, for in due season we shall reap if we do not lose heart. Galatians 6:9

_____

_____

_____

_____

_____

_____

_____

_____

_____

_____

_____

_____

_____

#16: YOU Have the Strength of Joy

The joy of the Lord is your strength.

Nehemiah 8:10

*Looking unto Jesus, the author and finisher of our
faith, who for the joy that was set before Him endured
the cross, despising the shame, and has sat down at the
right hand of the throne of God.*

Hebrews 12:2

Today you get two scriptures, so you know this devotional
is double the power! The YOU God created is designed
to operate in an indescribable strength called joy. Every
Christian needs this inner power to walk with victory on
this earth.

First, you must understand that the spiritual force of
joy is completely different from feeling happy. Happiness
is a feeling that you have when something good happens
to you. Happiness is flighty and is completely dependent
upon outward circumstances.

But, joy is an entirely different kind of power. This
force resides deep down on the inside of you and gives you

unmistakable strength, no matter what the outside circumstances are. It was Jesus' joy that enabled Him to endure a torturous crucifixion, separation from God, and three days in the pit of hell. Yes, He despised the shame, but His joy carried Him through to the victory until He was able to sit down at the right hand of God. And, the best news of all is in John 15:11, Jesus promises us that He has given us His joy!

This means when you lose your job, or the doctor gives a grim report, or your teenager has walked away from God, or you are walking through an intense season of emotional turmoil, you can still experience the strength of joy deep down on the inside. Sure, you might be despising the situation, but like Jesus did in His hardest trial, you can step out upon the strength of the joy of the Lord. No matter what you are facing today, there is joy available to YOU!

BELIEVE IT

In what area of your life is there stress, fear, or anger? These emotions rob you of all your strength and cause you to feel weak and out of control. Instead, release those issues to God. Begin to draw on the strength of JOY that comes from God's Spirit residing within you. Remember, joy isn't happiness…it's a spiritual force!

SAY IT

Father, I believe You have equipped me with the strength of joy. Help me today to trust in the promises of Your Word, so I can access that power of joy.

READ IT

They will enter Zion with singing; everlasting joy will crown their heads. Gladness and joy will overtake them, and sorrow and sighing will flee away. Isaiah 35:10 (NIV)

These things I have spoken to you, that My joy may remain in you, and that your joy may be full. John 15:11

Until now you have not asked for anything in my name. Ask and you will receive, and your joy will be complete. John 16:24 (NIV)

#17: YOU are a Success

Roll your works upon the Lord [commit and trust them wholly to Him; He will cause your thoughts to become agreeable to His will, and] so shall your plans be established and succeed.

Proverbs 16:3 (AMP)

Everybody is looking for success. If you Googled "how to find success" right now, 1.6 billion results would pop up in seconds. Thousands of books have been written on the topic and even more YouTube videos have been created; all of them promise a level of success if you follow their advice. But, what is success? And, how can we truly measure it? Is there even a way to measure success?

As with everything in life, we must look to the Bible to find answers to these questions. It's interesting that nowhere in the scriptures does God offer an exact picture of what "success" looks like. No particular level of achievement. No bull's eye salary. No detailed checklist for us to complete. He simply says to roll every aspect of our lives upon Him, to trust wholly in Him, and then our plans will be established and succeed. The end.

What if success was simply when your life is fully engaged with God, completely trusting in Him for your every need? What if your level of success was only judged upon your ability to be free to be the YOU He created? Because, when you are living each day as an authentic expression of the YOU He planned before the foundation of the earth, you will be filled with an unmistakable sense of fulfillment and tranquility. So much of our stress is a result of our striving to achieve tangible markers of success in every area of our lives. Instead, let's use that energy to draw closer to God, to trust in Him, and to allow Him to help us feel good about WHO we are becoming in Christ. When we are at peace with God and with ourselves, we will sense a deeper level of success than the world can ever give or ever take away.

BELIEVE IT

How do you measure success? Is it merely by your outward achievements or do you factor in the successes of your character, your service to others, or your relationship with Jesus? Today, meditate on the areas where you've experienced God's success in your life. Allow Him to encourage you to be the YOU He created.

SAY IT

Father, I believe You have laid forth a life of success for me: success in my soul, my mind, my body, my relationships, and my career. Help me to view success the way You view it. Help me to value the things You value. I trust in You completely and know You will cause me to find the deep sense of fulfillment and peace that can only come from You.

READ IT

Blessed is the one who does not walk in step with the wicked or stand in the way that sinners take or sit in the company of mockers, but whose delight is in the law of the Lord, and who meditates on his law day and night. That person is like a tree planted by streams of water, which yields its fruit in season and whose leaf does not wither— whatever they do prospers. Psalm 1:1-3 (NIV)

But remember the Lord your God, for it is he who gives you the ability to produce wealth, and so confirms his covenant, which he swore to your ancestors, as it is today. Deuteronomy 8:18 (NIV)

Trust in the Lord with all your heart and lean not on your own understanding; in all your ways submit to him, and he will make your paths straight. Proverbs 3:5-6 (NIV)

#18: YOU Can Lack Nothing

> *My brethren, count it all joy when you fall into various trials, knowing that the testing of your faith produces patience. But let patience have its perfect work, that you may be perfect and complete, lacking nothing.*
>
> *James 1:2-4*

Wow! What a promise to think that we can be perfect and complete, lacking nothing! We'd all love for that to come to pass in our lives, right? The only problem is the first verse of this scripture...the falling into various tests and trials part. Don't you wish you could become "perfect and complete" without all the hardships? But the truth is, for you to BE YOU, and to discover the YOU God created you to be, it's going to take some effort and some serious patience.

Life is hard and there are tests and trials to be faced. There's just no way around this fact. We live in a world that is cursed and there will always be resistance because you have an enemy who is opposing your progress to be the authentic YOU. If you have the belief that life should be easy, or that because you're a Christian, you shouldn't face hardships, you'll always be coming from the wrong premise. And, you'll always be frustrated, wondering why the world is attacking you.

BUT, if you will count it joy, knowing that there is purpose to the trials, suddenly your entire perspective changes. Instead of having a victim mentality that says, "Why is this happening to me?" you can rise up on the inside with a victor's mentality that says, "Bring it on, devil! This test is only going to make me stronger and better than before!" Instead of feeling defeat, you will sense the endurance and strength that comes from that spiritual force of joy.

You cannot control some of the tests that come your way, but you can control your attitude. And when you count it joy, you can overcome, and pretty soon you'll find you are on your way to being perfect and complete, lacking nothing!

BELIEVE IT

Today, make an effort to keep this scripture rolling around in your mind. Believe that God will use every circumstance, whether bad or good, to develop you into who He designed you to be. And when a trial comes, attack it with a victor's mentality!

SAY IT

Father, I believe You have given me the patience and endurance to face any test or trial that comes my way. While You don't cause bad things to happen, You certainly can use them to make me stronger. Thank You for Your power working in me today.

READ IT

The Lord is my shepherd, I lack nothing. He makes me lie down in green pastures, he leads me beside quiet waters, he refreshes my soul. He guides me along the right paths for his name's sake. Psalm 23:1-3 (NIV)

Let perseverance finish its work so that you may be mature and complete, not lacking anything. If any of you lacks wisdom, you should ask God, who gives generously to all without finding fault, and it will be given to you. James 1:4-5 (NIV)

Keep your lives free from the love of money and be content with what you have, because God has said, "Never will I leave you; never will I forsake you." Hebrews 13:5 (NIV)

#19: YOU are Healed

By His stripes we are healed.

Isaiah 53:5

When God created YOU, He created your body, mind and soul to live in perfect harmony forever. In that original plan there was no sickness, no disease, no fear, no depression, no decay. Mankind was to be one with the living God, united; and for this reason, no disease could be present. Then Adam allowed sin to enter into the world and all this changed.

There is so much that could be said about this, but for this devotional, let me stress this point: It was never God's plan for you to be sick in any way. It couldn't be, because God is only light, life, and love. He couldn't create sickness, even if He wanted to! Everything He touches gets healed and restored…and we saw this throughout the ministry of Jesus' earth walk. Everywhere Jesus traveled, He went about healing all people of every kind of sickness and disease.

Jesus came to live, to die, and to be resurrected so that YOU could be saved, healed, and restored. This was God's will for mankind when He created us. It was His will throughout the generations, and it is still His will for you and me today. Healing was, is, and will be His will forever. Jesus is the same yesterday, today, and forever!

YOU can believe for healing in your body, soul and mind. Whatever healing you need, you can rest assured that it is God's desire for you to be free and to live your life whole. Granted, there are times we must hold on to that healing by faith, and seasons when we must seek to find answers in the natural. But, even in that, YOU—the you that is saved and united with Jesus—are healed. It might take some time for your body to align itself with that truth; nevertheless, it doesn't make that truth any less true. If you are believing for healing, hold on to God's promise and don't let go. God loves you dearly, and wants you to experience the fullness of healing in every part of your life.

BELIEVE IT

If you need healing today, meditate on the promises of God. Revive your faith daily as you speak those scriptures over your life. See yourself healed, and thank God for His gift of health. Ask others to pray in agreement with you. And then, be patient.

SAY IT

Father, I believe You have healed my body, mind and soul. I speak Your healing in every part of my being, and I call myself "healed"! Even when I'm feeling pain and oppression, help me to hold on to the promises in Your Word. Help me to have peace in my heart, knowing You have already provided my healing.

READ IT

Worship the Lord your God, and his blessing will be on your food and water. I will take away sickness from among you. Exodus 23:25 (NIV)

Heal me, O Lord, and I will be healed; save me and I will be saved, for you are the one I praise. Jeremiah 17:14 (NIV)

He said to her, "Daughter, your faith has healed you. Go in peace and be freed from your suffering." Mark 5:34 (NIV)

#20: Where is Your Focus?

I press on, that I may lay hold of that for which Christ
Jesus has also laid hold of me. Brethren, I do not
count myself to have apprehended; but one thing I do,
forgetting those things which are behind and reach-
ing forward to those things which are ahead, I press
toward the goal for the prize of the upward call of God
in Christ Jesus.

Philippians 3:12-14

The ability to focus is huge. In fact, I believe it is THE key to be a successful person. What you focus "on" defines what you focus "out". The Apostle Paul understood this, as he was passionate to focus on the one thing that mattered: the plan of God. He was determined not to let his doubts, what happened yesterday, or even the circumstances he was presently in, deter him from focusing on the goal for the prize of his calling. And guess what? He finished his race strong.

There are countless situations and negative influences that will bombard you on a daily basis. But, what you choose to focus on will determine your success. If you focus on the promises of God and what you need to do to improve your marriage, your health, your business, or whatever you are going after, then you will move toward that upward call. If you keep your focus on the problem, or even if you turn your focus on things that help you escape from the circumstance, then you'll never find the energy to do what it takes to get you where you want to go.

Turn off the TV. Turn off the "Constant Negative News." Turn off the thoughts that are brooding on the worst-case scenario. Turn off the conversations coming from people filled with doubt and unbelief. Forget the failures of the past. Forget the facts of what happened yesterday. Decide to take on a fresh mental attitude and listen instead to the voice of your Heavenly Father. Turn your focus on the blessing of God and the promises in His Word. Focus on prayer. Focus on praise and worship. Focus on thankfulness. Focus on hope. This focus will move you toward your upward call!

BELIEVE IT

What is stressing you out right now? You cannot be the authentic YOU when you are under these burdens of stress.

Turn your focus upon a positive outcome and meditate on how you will find success in that area.

SAY IT

Father, I believe You have given me the ability to focus and give attention to Your Word and Your ways. Help me, by Your Spirit, to keep my focus on the hope of Your promises today. I believe You are giving me divine wisdom to move me towards Your perfect will for my life.

READ IT

Turn my eyes from looking on worthless things; and give me life in your ways. Psalm 119:37 (ESV)

Set your minds on things that are above, not on things that are on earth. Colossians 3:2 (ESV)

But the one who endures to the end will be saved. Matthew 24:13 (ESV)

#21: YOU Compare to No One Else

Let everyone be sure that he is doing his very best, for then he will have the personal satisfaction of work well done and won't need to compare himself with someone else.

Galatians 6:4 (LB)

Comparison. It's something we all do and it's never to our benefit. Either we're comparing ourselves with someone who is "worse off" than us so we can feel better about ourselves (this only breeds haughtiness), or we're comparing to others who are "better off" than we are so that we can feel bad about ourselves (which fills us with insecurity). Comparison is a lose/lose situation, and is one of the biggest traps by the enemy to keep you dissatisfied with the YOU God created you to be.

I remember being a ten-year-old boy, growing up in Spanaway, and the older boy next door just seemed so cool to me. He had good grades, was a good wrestler, had his letterman's jacket, and I remember thinking, "Wow. I'll never be that good. So why even try?" Ten years old! Where did I get that thinking at such a young age? Certainly not from my Father in Heaven. That kind of thinking can only come from the devil. Maybe you can relate.

Comparison will only hold you back. It will make you think, "Hey, I'm doing pretty good. I don't need to try to go further in my destiny." Maybe even, "I've done my share of good deeds; let someone else meet the needs of that person." Or on the other spectrum, "I'll never be able to have a marriage that good, so why don't I just give up on the one I have now?" Or, "I'll never be able to reach as many people as the pastor, so why should I attempt to help one?" Again, it's lose/lose!

You will never be YOU if you're trying to be someone else. You've got to come to believe that YOU are valuable and YOU are enough. Someone else's "enough" is not a better "enough". Your level of success isn't to be compared to another's, just as theirs is not to be compared with yours. God chose you to live YOUR life. Own that. BE that. Rejoice in who YOU are right here, right now.

BELIEVE IT

Have you been comparing yourself to anyone? Well, stop it! Today, meditate on the areas of your life where you have seen positive growth. Celebrate that and do not compare it with anyone else.

SAY IT

Father, I believe You have made me to be unique. Thank You that You do not compare me to anyone else or expect me to be anyone except me. Help me to love and accept the *me* You've created.

READ IT

Not that we dare to classify or compare ourselves with some of those who are commending themselves. But when they measure themselves by one another and compare themselves with one another, they are without understanding. 2 Corinthians 10:12 (ESV)

Let us not become conceited, or provoke one another, or be jealous of one another Galatians 5:26 (NLT)

Do nothing from selfish ambition or conceit, but in humility count others more significant than yourselves. Philippians 2:3 (ESV)

_____

_____

_____

_____

_____

_____

_____

_____

_____

_____

_____

_____

#22: YOU are Excellent — Part 1

> *O Lord, our Lord, your majestic name fills the earth!*
> *Your glory is higher than the heavens. When I look at*
> *the night sky and see the work of your fingers—the*
> *moon and the stars you set in place—what are mere*
> *mortals that you should think about them, human*
> *beings that you should care for them? Yet you made*
> *them only a little lower than God and crowned them*
> *with glory and honor.*
>
> *Psalm 8:1,3-5* (NLT)

When King David wrote these words, he was looking around in awe at creation and said, "Wow, God, you are excellent!" Then, right on the heels of this came the realization that this majestic, excellent God chose to create man just a little lower than Himself, and to crown him with glory and honor. This is YOU! Everything God made is excellent, and this means you are a part of that excellence. YOU were designed by God to excel in every aspect of your life.

Being excellent doesn't mean you have the perfect house or car, or that you've achieved a certain level of monetary success, or even that all your socks are expertly folded according to color in your drawer. Excellence is an attitude, a way of thinking and believing, that causes you to rise above the negative challenges and pressures that assault you on a daily basis. Instead of having a pity party or reacting in anger, an excellent person decides to rise above the circumstance, chooses to walk in joy anyway, and does what is needed to be done.

Excellence is getting the Word of God so deeply in your heart and mind that when you meet up with an issue, you respond like Jesus would respond, not how a victim would respond. When the bankruptcy comes, excellence says, "God will help us rebuild and overcome." When the doctor gives a bad report, excellence says, "I believe I am healed and I will walk through this with God's abundant strength." Don't get me wrong, being excellent doesn't mean you won't feel the blow of intense emotions sometimes… but, it does mean you don't allow yourself to wallow in them. An excellent person feels the pain and then takes it to God. Through prayer and relationship, an excellent person chooses to move forward.

BELIEVE IT

You CAN be excellent because YOU were made in the image of an excellent God. Meditate on this truth today.

SAY IT

Thank you, Father, for all Your excellence, even in me. I believe as You enable and empower me, excellence fills every part of my life.

READ IT

Who among the gods is like you, Lord? Who is like you—majestic in holiness, awesome in glory, working wonders? Exodus 15:11 (NIV)

Great is the Lord! He is most worthy of praise! No one can measure his greatness. Psalm 145:3 (NLT)

Sing to the Lord, for He has done excellent things; this is known in all the earth. Isaiah 12:5

#23: YOU are Excellent—Part 2

Then this Daniel distinguished himself above the governors and satraps, because an excellent spirit was in him; and the king gave thought to setting him over the whole realm.

Daniel 6:3

This concept of becoming excellent is so important, one devotional on this topic is not enough. Because to be YOU, the authentic YOU God created, you must begin to see yourself correctly and to believe you really can live every area of your life in an excellent way. Remember, being excellent does not mean being flawless. No one on earth can be that. But, everyone can learn to be excellent. Daniel was a man who sought to have an attitude of excellence in everything he did; and eventually, he was put into a position of great authority because of it!

Here's the great news: no matter where you are in life, YOU can be excellent right now. You don't have to wait until you've matured to a certain degree or your circumstances have reached a certain level of success. You can choose to be excellent TODAY. And even greater news…your level of excellence can only be compared to YOU. It's doing your best today. It's pushing your average today. God's not asking you be "as good as" someone else, He's only asking you to be as good as YOU can be today.

Knowing this takes such pressure off because when we hear teaching like this, we tend to disqualify ourselves thinking, "I'll never hit that mark, so why even try?" But "that mark", or that measuring stick, is between you and God, not anyone else. He's not asking you to be perfect, He's just calling you to an excellent life. Talk to God and ask Him where you could take a step forward in excellence. Is it on your job? Is it how you speak to your spouse? Is it how you treat your kids? Is it letting go of negative addictions that are holding you back? Whatever it is, you can trust Him that He will give you the power and the desire to take a step forward in that area of life.

Choose to be excellent TODAY. Then, do it again tomorrow. And, the next day. Pretty soon, you will be walking through every day with an attitude of excellence.

BELIEVE IT

In this prayer time, see yourself operating in a spirit of excellence in an area that normally pulls you down. Believe you have what it takes to overcome.

SAY IT

Father, I believe You have made me to be an excellent person and that I can walk in every area of my life in an excellent way. Thank You that today You are giving me Your power and strength to step forward in those areas I have been weak in.

READ IT

You are the most excellent of men and your lips have been anointed with grace, since God has blessed you forever. Psalm 45:2 (NIV)

I have heard of you, that the Spirit of God is in you, and that light and understanding and excellent wisdom are found in you. Daniel 5:14

Finally, brothers and sisters, whatever is true, whatever is noble, whatever is right, whatever is pure, whatever is lovely, whatever is admirable—if anything is excellent or praiseworthy—think about such things. Philippians 4:8 (NIV)

#24: YOU are Not a Failure

*He who covers his sins will not prosper, but whoever
confesses and forsakes them will have mercy.*

Proverbs 28:13

No one likes to fail. No one revels in the feelings of missing
the mark or of facing a mistake, big or small, public or pri-
vate. But, the truth is, every single one of us will experience
failure of some kind at some point in our lives…and prob-
ably on multiple occasions. However, take heart! Besides
Jesus, is there any person in the Bible who sailed through
their life without making a few (and oftentimes HUGE)
blunders along the way? And, these are our faith heroes!

The biggest truth you must hold in your heart when you
find yourself facing failure is this: you may have failed, but
YOU are not a failure. You are still a child of God who is
loved unconditionally by your Father in heaven. YOU still
have a destiny and a hope. And, as long as you don't cover
up and hide your mistakes (as the scripture above teaches),
you will be able to find mercy and forgiveness. God is way
bigger than your failure and He can take your mistakes and
use them as platforms for you to rebuild. Only God is crea-

tively powerful enough to take the cake in which you put all the wrong ingredients, bake it, and still make it taste good.

Obviously, depending upon the situation, it might take time and much effort on your part to turn everything around. Restoring anything valuable is hard work. But, never forget you are not alone. You have the strength of Christ working on the inside of you to help you endure the sting of failure, all the way to victory. And, as the scripture above encourages, live your life openly with those who are close friends. Be honest about your struggles and allow them to link arms with you as you fight the good fight of faith.

Remember, a failure is never the end...as long as YOU get back up.

BELIEVE IT

Is there any failure you have been afraid to admit? Any sin you have been hiding? First, talk to God about it and ask for forgiveness. Then, forgive yourself. Determine that failure will not define you. Finally, talk with a mature Christian friend who can help you walk through to victory.

SAY IT

Father, I believe that You love me, even when I've failed. Thank You for Your faithfulness to me, even when I've been faithless. Help me today to rise above this failure and to walk forward to victory.

READ IT

For a righteous man falls seven times and rises again. Proverbs 24:16 (AMP)

Therefore, if anyone is in Christ, he is a new creation; old things have passed away; behold, all things have become new. 2 Corinthians 5:17

I focus on this one thing: Forgetting the past and looking forward to what lies ahead, I press on to reach the end of the race and receive the heavenly prize for which God, through Christ Jesus, is calling us. Philippians 3:13-14 (NLT)

_____

_____

_____

_____

_____

_____

_____

_____

_____

_____

_____

_____

#25: It's up to YOU

Blessed be the God and Father of our Lord Jesus
Christ, who has blessed us with every spiritual blessing
in the heavenly places in Christ.

Ephesians 1:3

This scripture brings such hope to us because of those three little words "has blessed us." Notice it does not say "will bless us." We don't need to plead with God to do something else for us. We don't need to perform perfectly hoping to bend God's will to bless us…He already has blessed us! And not with just a few meager blessings, but with every spiritual blessing that can be offered from heaven!

The reason this can infuse you with intense hope is because right now YOU possess every ability you need to be the YOU God has called you to be. You don't have to wait on God to do anything else…He's done it! God's part is finished, and now it's up to you to learn to receive and to walk in what He's already done for you.

Here's an example: If a marriage is rocky, there is nothing from the outside that can be added to make that relationship good. There is no pill, no potion, no external ingredient to save the marriage. When two people make a decision to walk together in love, patience, acceptance, and forgiveness the relationship will change. Nothing needs to be added to the marriage, it is just husband and wife drawing from within the strength that was already there to make the relationship strong and healthy.

And, so it is with YOU. God has already put within you everything you need to live a fulfilled and blessed life. You don't need anything added to you. You don't have to wait for God to move. YOU are good to go…TODAY. You simply need to draw near to God, learn to live by His strength, and learn to believe and receive all that He wants to bless you with!

BELIEVE IT

Meditate today on the fact that the life of Jesus, living on the inside of you is filled with all the strength, hope, faith, and spiritual blessing that you will ever need.

SAY IT

Father, I believe You chose me before the creation of the world, and have accepted me just as I am TODAY. I believe that through Jesus and His life that lives in me, You have already blessed me with all You have to offer. Thank You so much!

READ IT

As His divine power has given to us all things that pertain to life and godliness, through the knowledge of Him who called us by glory and virtue, by which have been given to us exceedingly great and precious promises, that through these you may be partakers of the divine nature, having escaped the corruption that is in the world through lust. 2 Peter 1:3-4

He who did not spare His own Son, but delivered Him up for us all, how shall He not with Him also freely give us all things? Romans 8:32

The Lord is my shepherd; I shall not want. Psalm 23:1

_____

_____

_____

_____

_____

_____

_____

_____

_____

_____

_____

_____

#26: Be YOU...Like Jesus

Most assuredly, I say to you, he who believes in Me, the works that I do he will do also; and greater works than these he will do, because I go to My Father.

John 14:12

Wow. What a promise Jesus gives us here. Greater works, really? It seems too awesome to conceive. However, when the Savior of the world declares His belief in us, I don't know about you, but I'm going to grab hold of those words and believe them!

What holds us back from believing this verse is we relate these words to visions of walking on water, healing every person, and raising folks from the dead. Those acts seem so far out of our league that we disqualify ourselves from the truth of this verse. But, what if we removed these magnificent images, and first and foremost, allowed Jesus' words to encourage us to BE like Him and to walk through life like He walked. Only when you can BE like Jesus, can you DO what Jesus did.

We all can aspire to be like Jesus, simply because of the fact that He was a human being who walked on this earth and faced the same issues we all face. Just like you and me, Jesus dealt with family drama, staff problems, financial pressures, and friendship betrayals. He even felt the emotional pains of stress, the loss of close friends, and of course, so much more than we will ever face. He had to wrestle with all the dysfunctions of life, but he never bowed down to them. He just kept looking to His Heavenly Father, speaking God's thoughts and overcoming it all.

YOU were created to be like God. Jesus came and walked on the earth to remind you who you really are. When you embrace this truth, it elevates the sense of who you are. You will believe you were made to represent God in your world…not to suffer and struggle through the pain and drama of life. You are to walk as Jesus walked, never bowing to those negatives that try to pull you down.

BELIEVE IT

Today when you are facing a trial, think, "How would Jesus respond to this?" Then believe YOU have the strength and courage to respond the same way.

SAY IT

Father, I believe the same Spirit that resided in Jesus now resides in me. Thank You, Holy Spirit, that You lead and guide me throughout my day. Thank You for divine wisdom, integrity, and strength.

READ IT

Yet in all these things we are more than conquerors through Him who loved us. Romans 8:37

For whatever is born of God overcomes the world. And this is the victory that has overcome the world—our faith. 1 John 5:4

Therefore be imitators of God as dear children. And walk in love, as Christ also has loved us and given Himself for us, an offering and a sacrifice to God for a sweet-smelling aroma. Ephesians 5:1-2

#27: YOU are a Giver

And the Lord God said, "It is not good that man should be alone; I will make him a helper comparable to him."

Genesis 2:18

In the very beginning, God in his perfect wisdom knew Adam would not be his best if he remained alone. God realized man would never be complete until there were two who were able to give themselves to each other, and share in their destinies together. Then, the first thing He says is, "Go and create more!" And, so it goes with YOU. You cannot be YOU without being involved with people, giving of yourself to people, and sharing your destiny with people.

It is only in giving of yourself, your heart, your gifts, and your talents, that you can even discover who YOU really are. Your giving defines who you are, and causes you to be YOU. Think about it. The funny guy is not funny at all until he gives his jokes and humor away. Before that, he's just as serious-minded as the next guy. A kind person isn't kind at all, until she offers a kindness to another. Before that, she's just as closed off as the next lady. A generous person isn't thought of as being generous until he actually gives gifts to someone else. Just thinking about who YOU are doesn't mean a thing...until you offer YOU to someone else. Now, all of a sudden, you are impacting the world around you, just by you BEING you!

This is why it's such a tragedy when a person says, "If I had more to give, I'd give it away." Or, "Once I have it all together, I'll start giving." But, they've got it all wrong! This line of thinking is robbing them from becoming who God has made them to be. It stops the flow of blessing in their lives; the blessing of giving, and the blessing of receiving.

YOU are a blessing TODAY. I know I've said this before, but let me repeat myself: You, right now, is enough! Don't wait to be "more" to give yourself away...the "more" you long for is only received as you bless others with the blessing of YOU.

BELIEVE IT

You have something to give. Don't wait until you feel you're "good enough" to offer it to someone else. TODAY reach out and be a blessing in the life of another. You'll discover yourself in the blessing!

SAY IT

Father, I believe You have created me to be a blessing to others. Thank You that You have filled me with the fullness of You so that I have more than enough on the inside to give out to all those around me!

READ IT

But now God has set the members, each one of them, in the body just as He pleased. And if they were all one member, where would the body be? But now indeed there are many members, yet one body. 1 Corinthians 12:18-20

And above all things have fervent love for one another, for "love will cover a multitude of sins." Be hospitable to one another without grumbling. As each one has received a gift, minister it to one another, as good stewards of the manifold grace of God. 1 Peter 4:8-10

Let each of you look out not only for his own interests, but also for the interests of others. Philippians 2:4

_____

_____

_____

_____

_____

_____

_____

_____

_____

_____

_____

_____

#28: The Gift of YOU

> *So (the lame man) gave them his attention, expect-*
> *ing to receive something from them. Then Peter said,*
> *"Silver and gold I do not have, but what I do have I*
> *give you: In the name of Jesus Christ of Nazareth, rise*
> *up and walk."*
>
> *Acts 3:5-6*

Being YOU is not just for you to feel good about yourself; it's also for you to give out to others. Jesus is wanting you to be confident in who YOU are so that you will reach out to the people around you who so desperately need a touch from Him. And here's the best news: Jesus is not asking for you to give what you don't have; He just wants the natural expression of who you are. Being you means God flows out of you.

In this scripture above, Peter does this: The lame man had been sitting and begging at the gate all of his life, and this day was no exception. He looked up to Peter, wanting some money. But, that is not what Peter had. Little did the man know that what Peter did have was so much better! Good thing Peter didn't disqualify himself and do nothing because he lacked what the man was asking for. Quite the contrary, Peter gave what he did have and it changed the man's life forever.

Never disqualify yourself because you think you don't have the right stuff to offer! What do you have to give? Do that! Just be YOU. Are you a host? Then host great parties. Your parties may create lasting friendships between people. Are you an encourager? Then write letters or send texts of uplifting words to people. Your message might be the only light they see that day. Do you love to work with your hands? Mow someone's lawn who can't physically do it, or change the oil in a single mom's car. Your act of service could be the thing that brings them hope.

Who YOU are today is enough. What you have to give RIGHT NOW is exactly what God is asking of you. No gift of yourself is too small to change the life of another. So, what are you waiting for? GO and BE YOU to someone who needs a touch from Jesus.

BELIEVE IT

Make a list of 2-3 things you are good at. Thank God for giving you the ability to do these things and then ask Him to show you who you can bless.

SAY IT

Father, I believe You have created me to be a blessing to others. I trust that You're not asking me to be anything except who You made me to be. Help me today to recognize who needs a touch from You. Give me the opportunities to reach out to those people and show them Your love.

READ IT

Heal the sick, cleanse the lepers, raise the dead, cast out demons. Freely you have received, freely give. Matthew 10:8

For we are His workmanship, created in Christ Jesus for good works, which God prepared beforehand that we should walk in them. Ephesians 2:10

Every good gift and every perfect gift is from above, and comes down from the Father of lights, with whom there is no variation or shadow of turning. James 1:17

_____

_____

_____

_____

_____

_____

_____

_____

_____

_____

_____

_____

_____

#29: The Church is For YOU

Not forsaking the assembling of ourselves together, as is the manner of some, but exhorting one another, and so much the more as you see the Day approaching.

Hebrews 10:25

Everybody wants to be a part of something. Why do you think there are such vast expanses of land throughout the earth, yet we just keep piling ourselves into cities? At the core, we don't want to be alone; we want to be close to people. This is an expression of our Father God. Even He didn't want to be alone, so He created people! And this is why He also created His Church. You cannot be YOU outside of being rooted and planted within a local church.

I know, I know. There are a lot of people out there who say, "I love God, but I don't want to be a part of the church." But, that's like saying, "I love basketball, but I don't want to be part of a team." You don't really love basketball; you just like going outside by yourself and shooting some hoops. If you love God, then you'll want to be part of what He is doing, and God is ALL about building His Church!

The truth is, to be YOU, you need the church. There is such power when people come together and focus their lives together. It's so dynamic when hundreds or even thousands of folks assemble, worshiping, singing, serving, and hearing the Word...all focusing together. There's such strength in that. This is why everybody loves going to a Seattle football game...there's so much focus, you can register it on the Richter Scale!

Who YOU are is encouraged when you're a part of a living church. Where else can you minister to the person beside you, effectively serve your community, AND send support (both financially and personally) to ministries around the world? Church gives you the big picture and the small picture of humanity, all the while exhorting you, growing you, and supporting you.

YOU must be a part of a team to become all God has for you to be. Sure, you can be saved and love God, but to prosper in ALL He has for you, YOU need the Church!

BELIEVE IT

Are you a part of a local church? If so, what can you do to become more deeply rooted into that church? Are you serving? If you are not part of a local church, find one near you. It's God's will for you to be rooted and planted in a local church.

SAY IT

Father, I believe You have created me to be a thriving part of a local church. Thank You for setting me amidst like-minded Christian people with whom I can be linked up and focused with as I walk through life.

READ IT

Those who are planted in the house of the Lord shall flourish in the courts of our God. Psalm 92:13

For as we have many members in one body, but all the members do not have the same function, so we, being many, are one body in Christ, and individually members of one another. Romans 12:4-5

There is one body and one Spirit, just as you were called in one hope of your calling; one Lord, one faith, one baptism; one God and Father of all, who is above all, and through all, and in you all. Ephesians 4:4-6

#30: YOU are For The Church

*There are different kinds of spiritual gifts, but the same
Spirit is the source of them all. There are different kinds
of service, but we serve the same Lord. God works in
different ways, but it is the same God who does the
work in all of us. A spiritual gift is given to each of us
so we can help each other.*

1 Corinthians 12:4-7 (NLT)

Every person has been given spiritual gifts. Did you know
that? YOU are filled with the power of God and He has
deposited spiritual gifts within you. You might not see
them as such because you're not "in the ministry" as a pastor,
apostle, or evangelist, but if you read the entire chapter of 1
Corinthians 12, you'll see there are many different kinds of
spiritual gifts and that everyone has been given some.

Here's why many Christians don't know the depth of
their gifts or understand how to operate in them: Spiritual
gifts are given to each of us so we can help each other. In
other words, we have been given these gifts so we can minister to people in and through the church. There are, in fact,
only two reasons spiritual gifts flows: to meet the needs

of the church, and to meet the needs of our community through outreach from the church. In order for YOU to flow freely and dynamically in your gifts, you must be connected to the church.

Jesus is all about building a thriving church, and when you are engrafted into a local church, YOU will begin to thrive. The flow of His Spirit that rushes through His Body becomes part of your life, and your spiritual gifts will begin to flourish. You'll begin to realize the depths of your gifts as you serve and give to others. In addition, as you get into the creative flow of God, you'll discover gifts that you never imagined resided on the inside of you! YOU will find your purpose, fulfillment, and deep satisfaction when you are serving and giving to the Body of Christ and reaching out to those in your world who are lost. This is the perfect expression of the YOU God created you to be.

BELIEVE IT

Today read through the entire chapter of 1 Corinthians 12, and meditate on those truths. Ask God to speak to your heart so you can be encouraged in the gifts you already know you possess, and to be quickened to new ways of serving others.

SAY IT

Father, I believe You have deposited spiritual gifts in me. Thank You for giving me the power and desire to use those gifts for the benefit of others. And, I believe as I reach out with my gifts, I will experience Your blessing flowing in my life.

READ IT

Having then gifts differing according to the grace that is given to us, let us use them. Romans 12:6

And He Himself gave some to be apostles, some prophets, some evangelists, and some pastors and teachers, for the equipping of the saints for the work of ministry, for the edifying of the body of Christ, till we all come to the unity of the faith and of the knowledge of the Son of God, to a perfect man, to the measure of the stature of the fullness of Christ; that we should no longer be children, tossed to and fro and carried about with every wind of doctrine, by the trickery of men, in the cunning craftiness of deceitful plotting, but, speaking the truth in love, may grow up in all things into Him who is the head—Christ—from whom the whole body, joined and knit together by what every joint supplies, according to the effective working by which every part does its share, causes growth of the body for the edifying of itself in love. Ephesians 4:11-16

A Note from Pastor Casey

During these 30 days, many wonderful truths have been sown as seed into your heart and mind. Now, follow through on them, meditate on them, let them affect how you live every day. You may want to read through this devotional again and again as you learn to love yourself as God loves you, and to be the person He created you to be. It's time that you...

be*you*